Over 700 Ways to Live "Just for Today"

Tom Garz

Published by TG Ideas LLC, 2021.

OVER 700 WAYS TO LIVE "JUST FOR TODAY"

First edition. January 14, 2021.

Copyright © 2021 Tom Garz.

ISBN: 978-1386442394

Written by Tom Garz.

Table of Contents

Disclaimers

This book is for information only and is not advice of any kind, especially not Medical and/or Legal Advice. The author of this book is a Non-Professional. Seek professional advice, as needed. This book is meant to help, but using this information is at your own risk. The author of this book has made efforts to make sure the referenced information is/was correct when the book was published. Efforts were also made to avoid plagiarism in this book by the writer. Any reference to any specific product or service is for information or example only and does not constitute or imply any endorsement, recommendation, or favoring by TG Ideas LLC. TG Ideas LLC does not assume any liability to anyone and hereby disclaims any loss, damage, disruption from any errors, omissions, perceived or actual unintentional plagiarism, whether such are caused by negligence, accident, or any other means. Additional Disclaimers are at https://sites.google.com/site/tgideas/ideas-for-products-or-services/disclaimer

Summary - I am not a Healthcare Professional. I wrote this book based on my personal learnings/experience and the References at the end of this Book. This book is for your information only and is not medical advice.

****

Chapter 1 - Introduction

On my Driver's License, it shows I'm an Organ Donor upon my death. I'd like most if not all of my remains to be "recycled" when that time comes. That action takes care of my body, but then I thought what about what I've learned in life? - particularly how I <u>best</u> learned how to live. Maybe someone could use that too, I thought – so I wrote this book. I hope you find it useful in some way – I did, just by writing it.

As background, I have found the Inspirational Essay Just for Today, I Will Try to Live Through This Day Only[1] very helpful in my life. The concept of living "just for today" is not new at all. This concept weaves in and out of history starting in the 1800s with songs, hymns, poems, essays, etc. This book builds on the concept of "Just for Today".

---

1.   https://quoteinvestigator.com/2012/07/26/just-for-today/

Chapter 2 – "Just For Today"

This Chapter gives you my Personal Guidelines on living that I <u>try</u> to have for myself. Life experiences have shaped the Guidelines I have today. My Guidelines give me perspective and guidance as my day and life go along. My Personal Living Guidelines were developed over many years, from various sources, and from much introspection.

My Guidelines help me be the best me I want to be. Of course, these are just Guidelines and I adapt these to fit the day I'm living in. I also don't do all of them all the time every day. Usually, one or the other guideline will come to my mind as the day unfolds and reminds me of the person I want to be. These Guidelines will I'm sure change as my years go on – and I'll add some and maybe remove some.

These guidelines also help me "Manage the Stressors" in my life which is the initial step in my own "Stress Management". I try to first "Manage My Stressors" then, if needed, use "Stress Management" techniques that seem to work well for me. One of my favorite Stress Management Tools is Deep Breathing for Relaxation. I've found that if I "Manage My Stressors" I don't have to do as much "Stress Management".

Just writing these Guidelines in my own words has helped me image the person I want to be going forward. I hope you find some of these useful in your life, too.

1. Just for Today, I will live in and for today only. I have enough to do just for today. If needed, I can break up my day into manageable pieces. I can also re-start my day if I want to.
2. Just for Today, I will try to be happy, upbeat, etc. even if I don't feel happy. Sometimes when I act happy, content, okay – I start feeling that way, too.
3. Just for Today, I will fit myself into this day. I can do it. I can adapt to what is and not try to make the day fit me. Others

5

will like this too since I will be easier to get along with.

4. Just for Today, I will try to challenge myself mentally, physically, and maybe spiritually. This is good for me since I grow from this. I want to be the best me I can be – or at least a better me than I was before.

5. Just for Today, I will try to help others if I can. Sometimes I can't and that's okay too. I can't help everyone and everything.

6. Just for Today, I will do some things I don't want to do – if it is of benefit to others or me. Exercise is an example of this. It is good for me. Helping others, if I can, is good for my soul.

7. Just for Today, I will try to get along with people and with life.

8. Just for Today, I will get up in the morning, get dressed, and have the best day I can.

9. Just for Today, I will try not to argue or fight with anyone or anything. If I think about quarreling, I will consider how much energy it will take doing so – and also whether it would do any good.

10. Just for Today, I will try to be nice to others and myself.

11. Just for Today, I will not criticize, shame, chastise anyone – including myself.

12. Just for Today, I will "fix" myself before I try to "fix" others.

13. Just for Today, I will try to "observe" others and life – and not "judge" others and/or what's going on around me.

14. Just for Today, I will try to improve and control myself - and myself only.

15. Just for Today, I will give it some thought and make a day plan. If needed, I will change plans for something more important. I'll do what I can on my day plan. Some days I can do more, some days less.

16. Just for Today, I will look at my progress, instead of what I

haven't done.

17. Just for Today, I will slow down and maybe even enjoy life.
18. Just for Today, I will not act hastily on impulse, if I don't have to. I will give myself time to make good decisions. If uncertain, I will wait for more information or insights, so I can make a good decision. I will also consider that sometimes I just have to "wing it".
19. Just for Today, I will try to relax and not always be on alert. I can learn to allow life to happen instead of making life happen.
20. Just for Today, I will try to look at the big picture as the day unfolds, remembering that I always have options.
21. Just for Today, I will turn around if I think I'm going in the wrong direction.
22. Just for Today, I will talk and listen to my God.
23. Just for Today, I will not be so afraid of the world around me. I can face up to whatever comes along today. I can be my own Hero.
24. Just for Today, I will try to make the world a little better.
25. Just for Today, I will let others be. If it is okay with them, it is okay with me. I will not "barge" into other's lives and "steam-roll" them into my way of thinking and doing.
26. Just for Today, I will not be so afraid of death and dying – my own and others. Fear enters in but I will sweep it out today – and live today.
27. Just for Today, I will not get all worked up about the littlest things.
28. Just for Today, what I do or don't do is enough.
29. Just for Today, I am enough.
30. Just for Today, I don't have to have everything "just so".
31. Just for Today, I will try to go at my own speed, when practical or possible.

32. Just for Today, I will stay on task as much as possible.

33. Just for Today, I will "chunk up" a seemingly overwhelming situation.

34. Just for Today, I will ask for help, if I need it.

35. Just for Today, I will seek professional help if I think I am depressed or others think I'm depressed.

36. Just for Today, I will take some healthy risks.

37. Just for Today, I will try to expand my "comfort zone".

38. Just for Today, I will smile at other people and maybe even myself.

39. Just for Today, I will consider other people's viewpoints.

40. Just for Today, I won't think I know everything.

41. Just for Today, I will think for myself, considering the "big picture", and do what's best for my children and me.

42. Just for Today, I will not be bullied, intimidated, coerced, etc. into doing something I don't want to do.

43. Just for Today, I will not be a victim of life circumstances.

44. Just for Today, I will not let my past determine my present or future.

45. Just for Today, I will not let my feelings overwhelm me.

46. Just for Today, I will feel my feelings and work with my emotions in a healthy manner.

47. Just for Today, I will not feel sorry for myself.

48. Just for Today, I will forgive others and myself.

49. Just for Today, I will not try to get others to like me. If they like me, good, but I won't beg for their approval of me.

50. Just for Today, I will realize that some people like me and some don't – and that's okay.

51. Just for Today, I will approve of myself and not be so dependent on other's approval.

52. Just for Today, I will just listen to others, not interrupt, and not try to "fix" others.

53. Just for Today, I will take care of my children and myself first.
54. Just for Today, I won't go looking for problems.
55. Just for Today, I won't feel obligated to please others so that they like me and accept me.
56. Just for Today, I will be myself and try not to be someone I'm not.
57. Just for Today, I don't have to be responsible for everyone and everything in the world.
58. Just for Today, I will be responsible for my children and myself first.
59. Just for Today, I will not try to control, coerce, manipulate, shame, or intimidate others to my way of thinking.
60. Just for Today, I will encourage others and myself.
61. Just for Today, I will not mold myself to what others want me to be.
62. Just for Today, I will not try to "read other people's minds" or assume anything. If I have questions, concerns, or doubts I will ask.
63. Just for Today, I will stand up for my children and myself.
64. Just for Today, I will not be afraid of others and/or life.
65. Just for Today, I will have my own life and let others have their own lives.
66. Just for Today, I will be around people I like and they like me.
67. Just for Today, I will not be so dependent on others
68. Just for Today, I will like myself and maybe even love myself. I will at least accept myself – just as I am.
69. Just for Today, I will approve of myself – who I am and what I do – and realize there is always room for improvement.
70. Just for Today, I will realize that some days go better than others do.
71. Just for Today, I will provide food, water, shelter, attention, love, and acceptance to my children and myself – and maybe

that's just enough.

72. Just for Today, I will not look for problems. If problems find me, I will deal with them at that time. Until then, I will just relax and live.

73. Just for Today, I will not spend all my emotional and mental energy on "fixing" other's problems and pains. I will keep energy for myself so that I don't burn out. There's only so much I can give others.

74. Just for Today, I will realize that some days I can give more than other days.

75. Just for Today, I will not devote my day to pleasing others. I might choose to do this short-term for some reason or another – but not long-term. "People-Pleasing" is not good for me long-term.

76. Just for Today, I will mostly protect my children and myself.

77. Just for Today, I will not get my self-esteem solely from "fixing" others, e.g. solving other's problems.

78. Just for Today, I will not let other's pains pull me down too.

79. Just for Today, I will not "turn myself inside out" for others. I am me and others are others. It is best if I just "be me".

80. Just for Today, I will see myself in others I admire and try to be more like them, yet not lose myself in the process.

81. Just for Today, I will realize that how others see me is probably not how I see myself. I will be open to other's comments, observations, suggestions, etc. for self-improvement. If their words are valid, I will consider a change.

82. Just for Today, I will have my own dreams of what I want to do, where I want to live, who I want in my life, etc. I will let others have their dreams, too, and encourage them on their way.

83. Just for Today, I will have the courage to say what I mean and

do what I say - even if others reject me.

84. Just for Today, I will not "keep others hostage" by my gifts, attention, etc. I will let others come in and out of my life as they wish. I don't want them to feel obligated to stay if they don't want to.

85. Just for Today, I will give gifts just as gifts for others to do with what they want. I will not expect a thank-you or any other kind of giving back. No strings attached.

86. Just for Today, I will expand my social network, if I want or need to. If it gets to be too much, I can always scale back to whom I want in my network most.

87. Just for Today, I will have my own values in life. My values might not be the values of others. I will let others have their own values and I will be me with my values.

88. Just for Today, I will consider other's opinions. I will just listen and not feel like I have to tell others my opinions and/or talk them out of their opinions. They can be themselves and I can be myself. This works out best for me.

89. Just for Today, I will be, above all, honest with myself and try very hard to be honest with others. This is the best policy for me, yet I know I can't expect honesty from others all the time.

90. Just for Today, I will say and show that I am sorry if I make a mistake that involves others. I will also forgive myself and move on.

91. Just for Today, I will determine my own quality of life and not compare myself to others. I will take actions to maximize my own quality of life and not interfere with other's lives.

92. Just for Today, I will not be like a "moth attracted to a flame" in "stalking" the news/politics and even people who are not good for me.

93. Just for Today, I will not be overwhelmed with life. If

something is too big and it is importantly urgent that I do it,
I will "chunk up" the big thing into more manageable pieces.

94. Just for Today, I will try not to be caught up in the drama of
others. I will be caring and supportive of others, yet I will
allow others to live their own lives however they do.

95. Just for Today, I will chunk up this day into hours, minutes,
etc. if need be – just to get through the day.

96. Just for Today, I will be content with my own version of God
or lack thereof. My God is personal, just for me. I will not be
bullied into other's beliefs nor will I try to proselytize others.

97. Just for Today, I will consider the option of just doing
nothing in a situation. Maybe "it" will take care of itself.

98. Just for Today, I will try to be less serious and enjoy life.

99. Just for Today, I will consider that maybe this is as good as my
life gets, at this time.

100. Just for Today, I will not overthink things.

101. Just for Today, I will try to keep it simple and not over-
complicate matters.

102. Just for Today, I will not let one bad experience ruin my day
or life.

103. Just for Today, I will not spread myself too thin.

104. Just for Today, I will listen to others. If they clearly say "No", I
will respect that and back off.

105. Just for Today, I will not try to make someone else into
something they're not – especially if they don't want to
change.

106. Just for Today, I will not bug people.

107. Just for Today, I will not hover, helicopter, or micro-manage
others. I will let them be. I'll ask if they need help or they will
ask for it. I won't keep bothering them.

108. Just for Today, I will be okay with others being sick and/or
old, especially those with chronic conditions. I will love and

accept them just as they are. I will not try to "fix" them. If fear and sadness creep into my mind about them, I will feel the feeling, and then let it go. I will just let them be.

109. Just for Today, I will be friendly to others. I will try to get along with people, as much as I can, without sacrificing my own self.

110. Just for Today, I will accept things, situations, and/or people I cannot change. I will let them be and move on with my own life.

111. Just for Today, I will make the best of what I have to work with. I don't have to have all the pieces or everything "just so". I'll work with what I have.

112. Just for Today, I will try to change the things, situations, people (me) that I can change. I'm not going to try to change others if they, themselves, don't want to change. I will leave them alone – respect them, care about them, but that's about all. I can be me and I will let others be themselves – I won't bug them about what they "should" or "shouldn't" do.

113. Just for Today, I will try to sort out what I can change in my life and what I can't. If I want to or need to, I will change the things or situations that I can do something about. I will leave the things, situations, and/or people I can't change alone, for the most part.

114. Just for Today, I will not expect others to "take care of me". I will try to live my life as it is and take care of myself as much as I can. I will ask for help if I need it.

115. Just for Today, I will not "run scared" for no good reason. I will not entertain irrational fears with no sound basis. I will challenge fearful thoughts and if they are not valid, I will just say "no" to these thoughts and move on with my day.

116. Just for Today, I will be who I am and do what I can.

117. Just for Today, I will not seek revenge if I feel like doing so. It

is not good for me and not good for others.

118. Just for Today, I will realize that I can't erase my real or imagined past.

119. Just for Today, I will appreciate it when things are going well and leave it at that. I won't go looking for troubles or something to feel bad about. I will let the good feelings last.

120. Just for Today, I will let myself be, as I am, and not be angry, ashamed, etc. of myself.

121. Just for Today, I will listen to my conscience, inner voice, etc. to guide my day.

122. Just for Today, I have all I need to live a good day.

123. Just for Today, I will want what I have today and be content and appreciative of what I do have.

124. Just for Today, I will be content with what I do and don't do today. Tomorrow is another day. I'll do the best I can today and that's good enough.

125. Just for Today, I will not strive for perfection. My best is good enough.

126. Just for Today, I will not feel like a failure. I might fail at something but I am not a failure as a person.

127. Just for Today, I will not try to prove myself to anyone just to get them to like me. I am good enough. If others do like me, that is great. If they don't, that's okay, too. I like myself and that's good enough today.

128. Just for Today, I will realize that some days go better than others do. Some parts of the day might go better too.

129. Just for Today, I will take healthy short-term actions to achieve my long-term goals.

130. Just for Today, I will consider that more is sometimes not better.

131. Just for Today, I can do a good job but I can't do a "perfect" job.

132. Just for Today, I can be a good person but I can't be a "perfect" person.
133. Just for Today, I will try to encourage/motivate others instead of criticizing/chastising them.
134. Just for Today, I will realize there are always options. I can look for them if I need to.
135. Just for Today, I will ask someone else "How's It Going" and just listen. Maybe by hearing them, I'll realize how good I've got it and my life is not so bad after all.
136. Just for Today, I will choose healthy ways to comfort myself instead of the "knee-jerk" reactions to stress like excessive eating/drinking, over-working, etc.
137. Just for Today, I will find peace and contentment, whatever that is for me. If I look for it and work toward it, I'll have a better chance of achieving it.
138. Just for Today, I will let this day unfold just as it is. If I need to do something, I will do it. Otherwise, I'll just let this day happen as is and work with it. Maybe I'll even enjoy today!
139. Just for Today, I will realize that "more" means just that – there is always more. Maybe today I will be happy with what I have already and not try to obtain or do more and more.
140. Just for Today, I will realize I can't "have it all". I get to choose who and what I want in my life today. I just can't have it all – it is too much.
141. Just for Today, I will do my best and let God/Universe do the rest.
142. Just for Today, I will not be afraid of my feelings/emotions nor will I let them control my day/life. Feelings/Emotions are normal. I will be aware of them and manage them in healthy ways.
143. Just for Today, I will not put off what needs to be done today. I can't do everything but I can sure do the important, and

maybe urgent, things. The keyword is <u>important</u>. Maybe everything doesn't need to be done right now. I can pace myself today. Tomorrow is a new day.

144. Just for Today, I can chunk up a hard day into manageable pieces. The same goes for a hard job/task. I can strive for Progress as the day goes along.

145. Just for Today, I will reward myself in healthy ways, instead of excessive eating, drinking, bingeing on something or someone, etc.

146. Just for Today, I will just let this day happen, instead of me trying to make the day how I think it should go.

147. Just for Today, I will consider the option of just giving up, after I've tried all I can think of. This will not be a hasty decision and probably not made in one day. I will at least consider it today.

148. Just for Today, I will stop when I get frustrated, instead of pushing through it and maybe making a situation worse. I'll take a break and try to get a better perspective of what's going on. Maybe then, the job will go easier and better.

149. Just for Today, I will appreciate my body, mind, and spirit. We come as a package – a complete unit – with all three components. They all work together to keep me alive and guide me through life. I will listen to my body, my feelings, and my inner thoughts as the day goes on. By doing so, I'll have a better day.

150. Just for Today, I will realize how much freedom I do have and appreciate it. Mostly, I'm free to choose to have a good day today and strive to keep it a good day. I can do this one day at a time.

151. Just for Today, I will not let anyone or anything get me down.

152. Just for Today, I will not let others deter me from my day's plans unless there is a good reason to do so.

153. Just for Today, I will not let other's lack of planning become an emergency for me, unless I choose to do so. I'll decide what to do or not do – and not be pressured into something I don't want to do or think unwise to do.

154. Just for Today, I will not let other's lack of self-care get me down and I will not try to "fix" them, especially if they don't want to change. I will instead love and accept them just as they are and maybe move on in my day to my own life.

155. Just for Today, I will not re-live my past regrets or bad experiences in life. I also will not fret about the future. I will take care of today and take care of myself today – just today – and stay in today.

156. Just for Today, I will try to "do no harm". I will consider other's feelings and perspectives today as my day goes along. I will adjust my words and behaviors accordingly.

157. Just for Today, I will try to be more loving and caring

158. Just for Today, I will try to forgive others and myself.

159. Just for Today, I will believe that I can indeed have a good day and that everything will work out. My day and everything might not work out as planned but I did my best and that's good enough.

160. Just for Today, I will be hopeful and cheerful instead of moping around.

161. Just for Today, I will try to brighten up my own life and the lives of others.

162. Just for Today, I will accept sadness as part of life as well as being happy and even joyous if the occasion calls for it. Feelings come and go and sometimes I have more than one emotion going on – and that's okay.

163. Just for Today, I will console others, and myself if need be.

164. Just for Today, I will try really hard to understand others, whether it be their words or their actions/inactions. If I don't

understand, I can ask for clarification.

165. Just for Today, I will allow others to love me and not push love away.

166. Just for Today, I will give as much as I can today to make it a good day.

167. Just for Today, I will think of my life as good and my day as good, instead of drudgery.

168. Just for Today, I will believe I am successful, if only for today. I am a success if I make progress today and not hurt anyone.

169. Just for Today, I will try not to take life or myself so seriously. I will try to do some "play" or "fun" activities, whatever that means to me. I will also consider humor today to lighten my day and perhaps for those around me.

170. Just for Today, I will only do one thing at a time and try to do that thing well. Then I will move along and do the next thing doing it well. That's how I plan to do my day today.

171. Just for Today, I will try to get a little better each day, be a little better each day, and live a little better each day.

172. Just for Today, I will live my own life today instead of trying to live in and through other people's lives.

173. Just for Today, I will do what I can today to feel good about myself at the end of the day. If I hurt someone along the way, I will say and act "I'm sorry". I will also forgive myself and try to learn from my mistakes.

174. Just for Today, I will not be afraid. If I become afraid, I can ask myself "Is "it" OK, and are you OK, *right now at this moment*?" Usually, the answer is Yes, so there's no need to be afraid at this moment.

175. Just for Today, I will not think about dying, since I'm still alive. I'll die when it is time to die. If I'm alive, it is not time to die.

176. Just for Today, I will try to be as calm as I can be today, since I

am more productive and happier when I am calm, relaxed, peaceful, content, etc.

177. Just for Today, I will be proud of what I do today and not look so much at what I didn't do. I did what I did well and that's good enough.

178. Just for Today, I will keep going even if I have trouble doing so. I will rest as needed, but I will keep going until the day is done.

179. Just for Today, I will remember that today is just one day, consisting of some hours and some minutes. Whatever I'm going through had a beginning and will have an end. This too shall pass. Let's make the best of today.

180. Just for Today, I will make the best use of what is in my power and take the rest as it comes.

181. Just for Today, I will realize that maybe I don't have to know everything to do my day. I'll learn what I need to learn today and that is enough. There is no need to overthink something to do it.

182. Just for Today, I will realize I'm not alone. Despite what I'm going through there are others just like me. I can find them and draw comfort from them just to get through this day, this hour, or this moment.

183. Just for Today, I will relax now and then. I will take a few deep breaths, step away from what I'm doing, and just "chill out" for a few moments. If I'm able to, I will then keep on going with what I was doing.

184. Just for Today, I will do some acts of kindness for others. I will also be kind to myself. I will allow others to be kind to me, too, and appreciate them.

185. Just for Today, I will allow some time for creativity, whatever that is for me. In that time, I can just let my spirit soar doing what it does to create. I will stand back and view my creation,

saying "Wow! – I did that"!

186. Just for Today, I will respect other's personal boundaries and also protect my own boundaries too.

187. Just for Today, I will find someone who I can safely "really talk to" about what's "really going on inside me" – not chit-chat about the weather, sports, politics, etc. – just a "gut level" conversation.

188. Just for Today, I will accept compliments, as well as give them.

189. Just for Today, I will not suffer needlessly. I will try to find a way out of my "suffering" and not accept suffering as my lot in life, punishment, redemption, etc.

190. Just for Today, I will accept that I cannot save everyone and everything all the time. I will be content in helping a few others and myself now and then.

191. Just for Today, I will be personally responsible for myself and let others be personally responsible for themselves. I can accept and give some help along the way – but in the end, each of us is responsible for our own selves. It works best that way.

192. Just for Today, I will live a good life – a life to be proud of.

193. Just for Today, I will realize that sometimes it is best to just be quiet and/or do nothing in a situation.

194. Just for Today, I will not be a "jerk".

195. Just for Today, I will try to be humble and not "full of myself".

196. Just for Today, I will keep going if I think I'm going in the right direction and am doing some good in the world. I'll check my "Personal Internal Compass" now and then to see whether I should keep on going, turn around, or stop altogether.

197. Just for Today, I will accept that I'm not going to do

everything all in one day. I did some yesterday. I'll do some more today. Tomorrow I'll probably do more again.

198. Just for Today, I will not keep "banging my head on the wall". I'll stop, put a "bandage" on my head, and do something different.

199. Just for Today, I will do the important things first.

200. Just for Today, I will not let another's opinion of me determine my self-worth.

201. Just for Today, I will try to be honest, open-minded, and at least consider being willing to do something or not do something.

202. Just for Today, I will keep showing up for each day, no matter what, until there is no more of me.

203. Just for Today, I will try to think before I act or speak.

204. Just for Today, I will try to be true to myself.

205. Just for Today, I will consider life similar to a "smorgasbord". I can choose to do some of this or that - and choose not to do some of this or that.

206. Just for Today, I will accept that some people are just like that and leave them alone - if I don't like what they're doing or not doing.

207. Just for Today, I will not get sick and tired of life. I will do something to change my life so that I like life.

208. Just for Today, I will <u>live</u> today, actually <u>live</u> today – not relive yesterday or think much about tomorrow. Today I'm alive and I'm going to live today. You betcha!

209. Just for Today, I will tell the truth, especially to myself.

210. Just for Today, I will try to do no harm anywhere to anything.

211. Just for Today, I will have the courage or at least act as if I have courage. Sometimes just acting courageously gives me courage too.

212. Just for Today, I will try very hard to keep my promises.

213. Just for Today, I will not cheat. It's just not good for me and for others.

214. Just for Today, I will treat others nicely and with respect. I hope others will do the same. I will not, however, let others treat me badly and/or disrespect me.

215. Just for Today, I will not judge others or situations in life as good or bad. I will also not judge myself as good or bad. Instead, I will accept myself, others, and events as-is.

216. Just for Today, I will try very hard to be dependable. If I can't do something on time, I'll let others know so they're not waiting for me.

217. Just for Today, I will forgive others and myself.

218. Just for Today, I will have my own personal integrity. This means a lot to me and it is something no one can ever take away from me.

219. Just for Today, I will take responsibility for my words and actions/inactions.

220. Just for Today, I will be patient with others and myself. I will also be patient with life as it is today.

221. Just for Today, I will be loyal to someone or something, if I believe it is deserved and proven. My loyalty is contingent on ongoing proof. If the "proof" changes, I will re-evaluate my loyalty.

222. Just for Today, I will be respectful of others and myself.

223. Just for Today, I will be tolerant of differences in other people and in life, in general.

224. Just for Today, I will have humility realizing I'm one of many on this earth – yet I am one. Conversely, I will not let others humiliate me – I will stop it right away.

225. Just for Today, I will try to be generous without giving away what I need or my family needs. Most of all I will be generous with love, compliments, acceptance, encouragement,

understanding, empathy, etc.

226. Just for Today, I will realize that what I hear, see, feel, etc. might not be reflective of what is really going on around me. Frequently, my perceptions are off. If I'm not sure about something, I can ask for clarification.

227. Just for Today, I will not make a big deal out of nothing.

228. Just for Today, I will trust, if that trust is earned and proven. My trust is contingent on continued proof of the worthiness of my trust. If I'm not sure of something, I can ask about it.

229. Just for Today, I will try to learn from other's mistakes and not make the same mistakes myself.

230. Just for Today, I will not take advantage of others. This is just not good for me to do and it probably hurts others too.

231. Just for Today, I will stick with others who are going through hard times, if only to offer acceptance and love. I will not support others who can take care of themselves – at least not for long. I will encourage them to take responsibility for their own lives.

232. Just for Today, I will try very hard not to be prideful or "full of myself".

233. Just for Today, I will be brave and be my own Hero.

234. Just for Today, I will not compare my "insides" with other people's "outsides".

235. Just for Today, I will give others and life the benefit of the doubt.

236. Just for Today, I will not let other's opinions of me bother me. I will listen and if their comments have validity, I will consider changing. If not, I will dismiss their comments and move on in my own life.

237. Just for Today, I will give up looking for other's approval, recognition, love, etc. in those people who are unresponsive to me. I will let them be and get on with my own life and let

others come to me, if they want.

238. Just for Today, I will check my motive(s) in doing or saying something. Am I trying just to get my own way? If so, I'll stop right there.

239. Just for Today, I will check whether I need an "Attitude Adjustment". If so, I'll adjust myself, instead of trying to "adjust" others.

240. Just for Today, I will not let others determine my self-esteem and/or my path in life.

241. Just for Today, I will choose what feelings to keep and which feelings to discard or dismiss. I can choose to be happy, as much as I can. If sadness, grief, anger occur – I can feel those feelings in healthy ways – and decide what to do about these negative feelings.

242. Just for Today, I will focus on what is good and what is working.

243. Just for Today, I will consider backing out of situations and people who are not good for my morale and me.

244. Just for Today, I will consider setting limits on how much I help others.

245. Just for Today, I will ask for what I want or need, instead of expecting others just to know this.

246. Just for Today, I will not expect so much of others. I will expect a good job of myself, however.

247. Just for Today, I will not think so much that I "deserve" this or that in life.

248. Just for Today, I will remember that if I "fall down" – all I have to do is "get back up" – and regroup. No shame. No blame. Just get back up and keep on going – doing what I was doing.

249. Just for Today, I will seek out what is good in my life.

250. Just for Today, I will not try to make things fit – if they just

don't fit. I can stop, regroup, and try something else. If nothing works, maybe the things just don't fit – and leave it at that.

251. Just for Today, I will be there for others because I want to – not because I "should" be there, am obligated to be there, and/or because others think I should be there. I will think for myself what to do or not do.

252. Just for Today, I will realize I'm not the savior of the world.

253. Just for Today, I will stay in my reality and decide what to do or not do on an ongoing basis.

254. Just for Today, I will realize that today is just one day of many. Today is as good as any other to make it a good day. Maybe I can average out my days to a good life.

255. Just for Today, I will consider that my small actions in life can make a difference. I'll try to help some in life but I can't help everyone and everything. My best is good enough today. I'll at least try today, though.

256. Just for Today, I will "go with the flow", "roll with the punches", etc. in most cases. I might not like something or someone today but it's not worth getting upset about. I can adjust to life as-is today. If I need to take a stand, however, I will do so. I prefer to go easy in life instead of fighting life.

257. Just for Today, I will realize that people are just going to do what they're going to do or not, whether I like it or not. They can do that without my permission. For today, I'll live my life and let others live theirs.

258. Just for Today, I will choose how I look at my day/life. I can mope around thinking of my day/life as a series of nuisances, sufferings, or inconveniences – or I can change my thinking to something more positive. The choice is up to me.

259. Just for Today, I will try various things to break out of my negativity – going for a walk, calling someone, painting a

picture, etc.

260. Just for Today, I will not do or say things at the expense of others.

261. Just for Today, I will not get all upset if things don't happen as fast as I want them to. I'll think "how important is it"? I'll try to relax and just let life happen at its own speed.

262. Just for Today, I will look at my "at least's", e.g. – at least it isn't as bad as it was, at least I have some time/money left, at least I still have my spouse and family, at least the pain isn't as bad today, at least my health is better than it was, etc.

263. Just for Today, I will consider my "not as bad's", e.g. – it's sure not as bad as it was yesterday, it's not as bad with my friends and family, it's not as bad as it could be, etc.

264. Just for Today, I will leave room for a loving God to work. Maybe God can do better than I'm doing. It wouldn't hurt to ask for God's help.

265. Just for Today, I will do my part – whatever that is today. I will do my fair share and let others do their part.

266. Just for Today, I will not let others Shame or Bully me. If I, myself, have Guilt over something I did/said or didn't do/say, I'll try to correct the matter.

267. Just for Today, I will uproot irrational beliefs from my past. They are clogging up the works. I will keep the parts of my past that are good for me today.

268. Just for Today, I will set aside what I think I know – and be open to what is going on around me – learning all the time.

269. Just for Today, I will realize sometimes I have to do "damage control" and/or "put out the fires" of the day. I'll do what's necessary on my part and let others do their part to handle the situation.

270. Just for Today, I will accept "less than perfect". I will, however, not get in the way of others trying to be perfect or do things

perfectly.

271. Just for Today, I will try not to plan the outcome, because I'm not 100% sure how things will work out, anyhow.

272. Just for Today, I will sometimes just "jump in" if the time feels right. I won't wait until conditions are "just right" – perfect conditions might not ever happen.

273. Just for Today, I will be open to "Maybe's". Some activities may not be right for others, but might be just right for me.

274. Just for Today, I will be open to the vast "grey area" between Yes and No in life. I'll explore my options, maybe ask for clarification, and decide what is best for me.

275. Just for Today, I will learn how to be assertive, if I need to. I can stand up for myself today. I have courage. If I need to learn how to be assertive, or even how to say No, I will learn this in some way.

276. Just for Today, I will visualize Positivity and Positive Things happening. It wouldn't hurt to hope for the Best ☺ and maybe plan for the Worst ☹.

277. Just for Today, I will stop fighting "Imaginary Enemies". I'm tired of doing that. Either my Enemies, if I have any, come out and be seen – or I will just let these Mental Figments evaporate on their own.

278. Just for Today, I will maybe Trust my Gut in making Decisions. Maybe even my Head and My Heart might agree on the best course of action. Wouldn't that be nice?

279. Just for Today, I will go around, under, over Obstacles in My Day. No sense in trying to get them to move. I'll just move on and let them be.

280. Just for Today, I will think twice before accepting the "Mission Impossible" presented before me.

281. Just for Today, I will "plant seeds" that will hopefully make things better instead of making them worse. I know when I'm

building up others and when I am tearing down others.
Today I choose goodness and hope for others and myself.

282. Just for Today, I will do things that are important to me, even if they won't make any money, they serve no purpose according to others, etc. I'll do what I want to do as long as what I do or say won't hurt others. I can be me and creative.

283. Just for Today, I will have limits and try to stay in balance – not too much of this and not too much of that.

284. Just for Today, I will be responsible for my young children, if any, and myself. I will let others be responsible for themselves. I will take care of myself first then I'll be in better shape to help others, if I think it best to do so.

285. Just for Today, I will not be coy and needy. If I want or need something, I'll ask for

286. Just for Today, I will not expect the world to revolve around me. I am part of a whole and I will act as such. I will give and take, just like everyone else. I will share and play nice together with others, just like we learned in Kindergarten.

287. Just for Today, I will realize that I really do have a good life and be grateful for what I do have.

288. Just for Today, I will not be dependent on others to determine my self-worth. I am a worthwhile person just as I am, whether others think so or not. I am me and that is okay.

289. Just for Today, I will just do my work and let others be.

290. Just for Today, I will be okay with a difference of opinion. I am me and others are others. I will be me and I will let others be themselves. I won't let me and/or others get me down. I will respect others and myself.

291. Just for Today, I will figure out how to handle difficult situations and/or people. I might have to learn some new skills, but that's okay. I want to live with others as best as I can.

292. Just for Today, I will try to tone down disagreements and not aggravate them. I will take a break from others and myself as needed or wanted. I will strive for a middle ground with others.

293. Just for Today, I will practice making it better, not perfect, just better.

294. Just for Today, I will try very hard to see what is good about it – or what is good about them. I will build on that. I will look for similarities instead of differences.

295. Just for Today, I will try to decrease something/someone who is not good for me – if I can't stop it altogether.

296. Just for Today, I will try to be loyal to my spouse and children. I will try to put them first above everyone and everything.

297. Just for Today, I will not let age hold me back from doing something I want to do. I might be viewed by others as too old or too young. What others think is not going to hold me back today from pursuing my hopes and dreams in life.

298. Just for Today, I will accept I am not a Miracle Worker. I just can't perform Miracles. I can, however, do my best and let the rest go.

299. Just for Today, I will try to think, talk, and act positively.

300. Just for Today, I will adjust and re-adjust, as needed, to what is happening in my day. I can do this just for today.

301. Just for Today, I will not take things so personally or seriously today. I will lighten up. Yes, I will.

302. Just for Today, I will just do it and be done with it.

303. Just for Today, I will realize I'm not at the mercy of others. I can think and act independently today. I have my own mind and I will use it. I will consider others but make up my own mind about what to do or not do today. I will also let others do the same.

304. Just for Today, I will consider experimenting with my day and my life. I can "think out of the box". I can try things and see how they work out.

305. Just for Today, I will try to keep an open mind to alternatives and options around me. I might just get insights from the least likely person, place, situation, etc.

306. Just for Today, I will consider that Enough is Enough and just quit what I'm doing or at least minimize something/someone in my life.

307. Just for Today, I will sometimes ask myself "Why am I doing this?" or "Why do it?" It's good to see now and then if I'm going in the right direction.

308. Just for Today, I will regroup after an emergency, if one occurs. I need this time to calm down and figure out what to do next.

309. Just for Today, I will try to "perk up" others, along the way. Maybe this will help me feel better too.

310. Just for Today, I will see how little I have control over. I do, however, have full control over my attitudes and myself. Might as well work on those.

311. Just for Today, I will realize that I don't have to be in someone else's "Soap Opera". I also don't have to create a "Soap Opera" for others to join. I can take care of myself and ask for help if needed.

312. Just for Today, I will not whine too much and expect others to "fix" me.

313. Just for Today, I will not overthink what to do next. I will do the next right action in front of me.

314. Just for Today, I will help others because in so doing I help myself.

315. Just for Today, I will be okay in and of myself.

316. Just for Today, I will not try to make sense of something that

just doesn't make sense, especially contradictory information.

317. Just for Today, I will not need to know everything about everything and everyone.

318. Just for Today, I will not need to gain something even if it is good. I don't have to have everything to have a good life. I will appreciate what I do have.

319. Just for Today, I will try to be tolerant of others and of life, in general. The world and all in it are just not here for me. Events happen whether I like it or not.

320. Just for Today, I will try not to react to other's "pushing my buttons". If I don't react, then maybe they'll get the hint that the "hot buttons" no longer work.

321. Just for Today, I will try not to be so "thin-skinned" or so sensitive to those around me and the events of the day.

322. Just for Today, I will try not to react, especially over-react. Instead, I'll respond, or not, to the people and situations today.

323. Just for Today, I will try to listen, evaluate, and learn more.

324. Just for Today, I will choose whether to be obedient – or not. I will not "blindly obey". I will decide what is best for my children and me.

325. Just for Today, I will choose not to be miserable today. Others around me might be miserable, but I will not. I'll try to find a way out of my misery.

326. Just for Today, I will not believe everything I hear or see, especially on the Internet. I will evaluate for myself what is real and not real – good or not good – etc. I will check "it" out as needed or wanted. I will then decide what to do, or not do, about what I have seen or heard.

327. Just for Today, I will see how in Nature very little "has to be", e.g. trees are flexible and not rigid; ants make paths around things, etc. Nature adapts to what is. I'll do the same today.

328. Just for Today, I will not engage in negative thinking like "No one cares", "What's the use?", "They will only take advantage of me", etc.

329. Just for Today, I will realize that then was then and now is now. I will live in the now.

330. Just for Today, I will not stay "stuck". I will look for ways to become "unstuck". If I need or want help doing so, I will ask for it.

331. Just for Today, I will avoid going where I'm not wanted or stay around people who don't like me. I'm worth more than that. Some people like me and some people don't – and that's okay.

332. Just for Today, I will realize that everything is temporary in life – situations come and go – people come and go – time comes and goes – life comes and goes. I will make the most of the time I have with each.

333. Just for Today, I will consider asking others how I can help, or how can I straighten this out, etc. I will try to harmonize with others as best as I can.

334. Just for Today, I will dismiss the thoughts that I am not good enough, I don't do enough, that my work is not good enough, I don't have enough, etc.

335. Just for Today, I will not let my self-worth be tied up in doing enough, being enough, looking good enough, having enough, etc.

336. Just for Today, I will check my actions as most people do, but I will defer from "second-guessing" myself on what I did or didn't do. I'll take responsibility for what I do or don't do. I'll do my best and that's that.

337. Just for Today, I will seek a balance between not doing anything at all, just getting by, doing enough and having enough, overdoing it. I will seek to be in the middle –

something I can handle.

338. Just for Today, I will not blame others for my own misfortunes – and not blame myself for other's misfortunes. I will take responsibility for my own life – and others are responsible for their own lives.

339. Just for Today, I will admit my mistakes, make amends, and move on.

340. Just for Today, I will take all the time I need to grieve losses. I will try not to wallow in grieving, though, at the expense of living my life now. If I need or want help grieving, I will ask for it.

341. Just for Today, I will be willing to do something I don't want to do – IF there is a good reason for doing so.

342. Just for Today, I will have the courage to do what I need to do or say.

343. Just for Today, I will be okay with uncertainty, even if I don't like it.

344. Just for Today, I will not get caught up in conflict, unless there is a very good reason for me to do so.

345. Just for Today, I will live with assurance and confidence, even if I don't feel that way all the time. I'm doing my best.

346. Just for Today, I will take some healthy risks, because it is good for me to expand my "comfort zone", lest my world get smaller and smaller.

347. Just for Today, I will have faith, trust, and hope in uncertain times that all will work out okay. I might not like how things are going – or how things turned out – but I will be okay with it.

348. Just for Today, I will face the unknown as best as I can. I will not hide from life, but rather have the courage to face whatever is in front of me.

349. Just for Today, I will be okay with change, if it is good for me

and/or my children. Some changes I don't have to participate in, some I do. If I have a choice, I'd just as soon choose to change or not.

350. Just for Today, I will accept differences in my life, as best as I can. Everyone and Everything is different in one way or another. Maybe I can even learn from differences.

351. Just for Today, I will not let depression get the best of me. Everyone gets "depressed" now and then for one reason or another. I will seek Professional Help if wanted or needed. In most cases, it's up to me to ask for help.

352. Just for Today, I will not fight back, unless I need to for my own safety or my children's safety. If I'm upset, I'll calmly decide what to do or not do. I'm in charge of what I do with my emotions. I'll not let people or events get the best of me.

353. Just for Today, I will do what I can or want - when I can - if I can.

354. Just for Today, I will realize that sometimes the demand exceeds my capacity – and I will adjust accordingly.

355. Just for Today, I will push myself a little bit to improve myself in some way or another. This helps me grow in life, which is good for me in many ways.

356. Just for Today, I will "get a life" – I will find out what I like to do and what I don't like to do. I will try to do more of the things I like to do and less of the things I don't like to do. This just makes sense.

357. Just for Today, I will retain what I find useful and helpful and discard/avoid that which is not. I can choose whom and what I want in my mind and my life.

358. Just for Today, I will *consider* that others might be "right" and I am "wrong".

359. Just for Today, I will "give it a try", "give it a whirl", etc. Why not? What do I have to lose?

360. Just for Today, I will remember that everything looks worse when I'm tired. After a good night's sleep, things might very well look better.

361. Just for Today, I will not spread my bad mood to others nor will I allow other's bad mood to pull me down. I will do what I can to improve my mood, whatever it takes.

362. Just for Today, I will at least consider help from others. Help might be just what I need and I don't know it. After consideration, if other's help is not wanted or needed, I will tell them so and thank them for their effort.

363. Just for Today, I will do what is important in front of me, especially if it is both important and urgent. Something Important might be to stop working and just listen to someone I care about, e.g. spouse, child, etc.

364. Just for Today, I will not worry about what might happen or not happen. If something comes up, I will deal with it.

365. Just for Today, I will accept and manage my limitations. Everyone has limitations of some kind. Today, I will do what I can. If others depend on me, I will tell them what I can and cannot do today.

366. Just for Today, I will back out of pointless disagreements, perhaps conceding that "you might be right" – or something like that - and ending the conversation or changing the subject.

367. Just for Today, I will live and learn. This is how I grow. If I'm not growing, I'm dying. I don't want to die. I want to live.

368. Just for Today, I will quit bothering others who don't like me, who don't want what I have to offer, or are not interested in what I have to say. I'll just leave them alone and seek out where I am wanted or needed.

369. Just for Today, I will not just wait to die....or wait until conditions are just right for me to start living. I will take what

I have today and work with it.

370. Just for Today, I will realize that I can't keep people/pets from aging and eventually dying. I will also realize that I cannot make someone better, especially if even the doctors can't do so. What I can do, instead, is love and accept them – and let nature take its course.

371. Just for Today, I will have something to look forward to.

372. Just for Today, I will not be so much in a hurry. I'll slow down, do a good job, and enjoy my day.

373. Just for Today, I will not be so afraid of everyone and everything today. I'll not look at everything and everyone as something I need to do something about. I will take events and people as they are today without the need to fix them or it. I will just let them or it be.

374. Just for Today, I will not look at everyone and everything as a "task" that I must do something about right now. I will just let people, things, events be and not feel responsible to do anything. I will wait for a "call to action" instead of just "jumping in" to fix it.

375. Just for Today, I will not waste my time and energy on things that are not important to me. I'll focus on whom and what is important to me today.

376. Just for Today, I will not live my day and my life according to what others want me to be and do. I'll consider what others want and decide for myself what is best for my children and me today.

377. Just for Today, I will look at the options around me. I will keep an open mind as the day goes along. I might need or want to change my day/life plans if something comes up. I'll remember that no matter what I have options.

378. Just for Today, I will consider, really consider, what others are telling me. Maybe my reality is just not valid. Maybe they see

things I don't see.

379. Just for Today, I will not be so fearful, based on my previous bad experiences in life. My past is just not going to determine my present today – I won't allow it.

380. Just for Today, I will not do everything to completion if I don't want or have to. Sometimes it's better to just stop and leave it as is. I'll decide as I go along today.

381. Just for Today, I will not feel like I have to "do it" because no one else is "doing it" and it "must" be done. I'll consider what all is at stake and decide whether I want to get involved or not.

382. Just for Today, I will let others be personally responsible for themselves. I will be responsible for my children and myself.

383. Just for Today, I will respect myself and my children – no matter what age they are.

384. Just for Today, I will compliment more than criticize. I will build up more than tear down.

385. Just for Today, I will accept failure in others and myself. Failure is a fact of life. Failure teaches me what does not work. I'll find out what does work.

386. Just for Today, I will not be afraid to fail, look foolish, or to take healthy risks.

387. Just for Today, I will not make fun of others or bully others because I don't like it when it happens to me. Before I act or speak, I will consider how I would like to be treated – and do similar.

388. Just for Today, I will not be defensive listening to what others say about me. If what they say has validity, I will take heed, and maybe do something about it. I don't have to prove myself to anyone – since I am okay with and in myself today.

389. Just for Today, I will not have such a "short fuse" or low tolerance to frustration. I'll make sure I have an adequate

emotional cushion between my "insides" and what goes on around me today.

390. Just for Today, I will try not to be so impulsive. I will be more deliberate in my words and actions. I'll think before I speak or act.

391. Just for Today, I will not quit prematurely. Everything has an end to it and I'll keep deciding whether to keep on going or when "enough is enough".

392. Just for Today, I will not be a "victim" of my day or life. I'll decide as my day and life unfold what to do next to take care of my children and myself. There are always options. I might have to ask for help, too. I'll think about it.

393. Just for Today, I will not let my perceptions of what others think of me determine my day or life. If I think something is wrong, I'll ask about it.

394. Just for Today, I will not have my day/life revolve around money – making money, saving money, keeping my money, etc. Yes, I need money but I don't want the pursuit of money to "rule" me.

395. Just for Today, I will keep on going. I might be discouraged or in pain, but I will keep on going.

396. Just for Today, I will be okay being alone. If I get lonely, I'll do something about it – call someone, be around people, etc.

397. Just for Today, I will not be so afraid of loved ones (people/pets/me) getting sick, getting older, and even dying. <u>When</u>, not if, but <u>when</u> something happens I'll deal with it then. I'll not fret about it until then.

398. Just for Today, I will not go "looking for troubles". I will be alert to changes and, if necessary, manage those changes/events at that time.

399. Just for Today, I will consider that maybe it's the way it's supposed to be. Maybe I don't have to do anything about it.

Maybe there is no problem, after all.

400. Just for Today, I will strive to be teachable – or at least consider what is being presented to me.

401. Just for Today, I will try to be more "freewheeling" and not take life so seriously.

402. Just for Today, I will thank people and events as they happen.

403. Just for Today, I will have free will to live my own life and I will respect other's free will to live their lives the way they want to.

404. Just for Today, I will stop negative spirals in my thinking and acting.

405. Just for Today, I will "curb my tongue" and use discretion in speaking and acting. Sometimes others don't need me to tell the "truth" of what I see them doing or not doing. Others might not want or like my "pearls of wisdom" for them.

406. Just for Today, I will not let others or events pull me down. I will protect my good thoughts and good feelings today.

407. Just for Today, I will look around me and see what a good life I have, what good friends/family I have, and all the help around me I need.

408. Just for Today, I will realize that cooperation or understanding from others is nice but is not necessary for me to move ahead. I will find a way.

409. Just for Today, I will say No, if needed or wanted. If I have trouble saying No, I will learn the skills to say No and stand up for myself.

410. Just for Today, I will realize I'm stronger than I think. When all else fails, I can rely on myself and My God to get me through this. Help and Support are wonderful, but not always available. I will get through this as best as I can with what/whom I have available.

411. Just for Today, I will consider the best thing might be to Be

Quiet, Minimize Contact, and Be Thankful.

412. Just for Today, I will live my own life and not wait for others to make a life for me.

413. Just for Today, I will realize that sometimes it is good to just "jump in" and take a chance.

414. Just for Today, I will realize that it is okay to have fun. I can have fun in my own way. I can experiment with finding out what I want to do for fun. I don't have to work all the time!

415. Just for Today, I will consider other's actions/inactions and decide what to do about them, if necessary. Sometimes I don't have to do anything. They can just be and I can just be. If we can't "be" together, I'll consider doing something about it.

416. Just for Today, I will ask for clarification, if needed or wanted. I'll try not to guess or assume something.

417. Just for Today, I will do a "little bit". "Little Bits" add up to Progress.

418. Just for Today, I will "spring back" when life throws me a "curveball". I'll readjust and move on. Life doesn't have to get me down for long. I'll find a way out of this.

419. Just for Today, I will not let my emotions bounce all over the place. I'll stop and figure out what is really going on – and try to find a way to manage my emotions. I'll not let my emotions determine my course in life or my day today.

420. Just for Today, I will be happy even if those around me are not happy. It's okay for others to be happy around me when I'm not, too. Sometimes I'm just not happy and that's okay. We all don't have to be happy all the time. Nice but not necessary.

421. Just for Today, I will pursue my own happiness and let others pursue theirs.

422. Just for Today, I will trust that my needs will be met today. I

probably won't get all I want today, but I'll trust that I will get what I need.

423. Just for Today, I will trust that "things will work out" somehow, someway.

424. Just for Today, I will just love and accept people as much as I can.

425. Just for Today, I will take life as it comes and adapt as needed or wanted. I can be flexible.

426. Just for Today, I will do my best and let God/the Universe do the rest. I can only do so much. Some things are out of my hands. Sometimes the results, too, are not in my control.

427. Just for Today, I will "experiment" with life – be creative, playful, "see what I can get away with", etc. I'll maybe discover I'm freer than I thought.

428. Just for Today, I will consider that many things are someone else's business and not my business.

429. Just for Today, I will give myself permission to "get involved" if I want to or need to. Sometimes I just don't want to get involved in something and that's okay too.

430. Just for Today, I will avoid self-pity, regrets, discouragement, etc. I'll not seek out company to be miserable with – or manipulate others to feel sorry for me. I might feel sorry for myself and that's probably okay for a while – but I won't "spread it around" or wallow in this mood. I'll find a way out.

431. Just for Today, I will not be so afraid of life and of people, e.g. afraid to live my own life, afraid to let others live their own lives as they wish, afraid of what others think of me, afraid to be myself, etc. I'm tired of being afraid and I'm going to take efforts to just stop being afraid of everyone and everything. If I need help doing so, I'll get help. This is important to me.

432. Just for Today, I won't be afraid to hold my head high – despite what I do/did or did/didn't do. I did my best at the

time and am trying to do better now. Maybe if I respect myself, others will respect me too.

433. Just for Today, I will not try so hard. I'll try hard but not hurt others or myself in the process.

434. Just for Today, I will do my best and encourage others to do the same. I'll stop doing things others can do for themselves.

435. Just for Today, I will realize that others do not have to think or act like I do. I won't expect others to do things "my way".

436. Just for Today, I will be aware that others don't have to treat me nicely and with respect. This is nice when it happens but I don't need it. If others treat me badly, I will consider what to do to stop their behavior or at least distance myself from them.

437. Just for Today, I will not engage with people who just want to argue or fight. Some people are like that. I, however, will decide whether I want to participate or not.

438. Just for Today, I will realize that I don't have to wait for others to respond all the time. If necessary, I will give them a deadline to respond and mean it. I can keep moving even if others do not.

439. Just for Today, I will realize that others do not have to cater to my wants, preferences, or needs. I will attend to my own wants and needs as much as I can – and ask for help as necessary.

440. Just for Today, I will stop abuse, resentments, revenge, etc. on my end. It's not healthy for me to hold on to a grudge or to allow people to continue to hurt me. I probably won't change the other person but I can sure change myself. I will protect myself, try to forgive them, and move on in my life.

441. Just for Today, I will stop others from hurting me, not let them hurt me in the future, and allow the hurt to heal.

442. Just for Today, I will not put my life on hold waiting for

someone or something to change. It's my time to live.

443. Just for Today, I will try not to "use" others to get what I want or to make me feel better, e.g. guilting/shaming others, keeping someone dependent on me, etc. If I can't stop right now, I will have an "exit plan" to do so.

444. Just for Today, I will give gifts with "no strings attached", e.g. expecting a thank you, expecting them to use my gifts in a certain way, etc.

445. Just for Today, I will be responsible for my death, and maybe my spouse's death, and not leave it to survivors to make decisions, clean up after me, etc.

446. Just for Today, I will get rid of the "shoulds", "musts", etc. from my life. Others can do what they want, but I'm not "shoulding" or "musting" myself or anyone else anymore.

447. Just for Today, I will manage other's disapproval of me. I will consider what they have to say and if it has validity, I will take heed. Otherwise, I will not let other's opinions of me get me down.

448. Just for Today, I will ask questions as needed. I will check with others occasionally to make sure "all is right" – if I'm not sure.

449. Just for Today, I will not try to "relive the past". It never is quite the same and all I do is end up frustrated. I can retrieve memories, if I want, but that's about it. The past has passed. I want to live in today.

450. Just for Today, I will not "personalize" other people's problems in myself. I will have compassion and empathy but I am me and they are them.

451. Just for Today, I will try very hard to work and live with others. I don't have to do it all myself. I can ask others to work with me on our common goals.

452. Just for Today, I will not "sit and stew" because someone else

is not "pulling their share of the load". I will try to straighten out the situation.

453. Just for Today, I will consider "what do I have to lose?" or "what's the worst that could happen" in making decisions as my day and life go along.

454. Just for Today, I will shield and protect my children and myself if there is a real danger. I will not be hypervigilant or hovering though about some imagined danger to us.

455. Just for Today, I will quietly "go about my business".

456. Just for Today, I will try, really try. I'll get up, get dressed, make my bed, and do something today, taking breaks as needed. I might get more done than I think I can do. I'll do my best.

457. Just for Today, I will consider how busy my family and I want to be today. We don't have to participate in the "busyness" around us, if we don't want to or have to. Maybe we'll opt for simplicity and just have fun today in simple ways.

458. Just for Today, I will live within my means. I'll not overdo frugality though and become a miser, thus hurting others and myself around me.

459. Just for Today, I will believe in healing. I might not heal but then again maybe I will. I'll cling to hope today and believe that I <u>am</u> healing, perhaps in miraculous ways.

460. Just for Today, I will wait for an answer if I don't have a good answer right now. I'll stay open to possible "answers" but not be too hasty to pick one. Sometimes answers are "right around the corner" or come in a way I didn't expect.

461. Just for Today, I will consider doing what I fearfully avoid, if it will help me and/or others. I have the courage and I will use it!

462. Just for Today, I will "talk" nicely to myself and encourage myself. Maybe by doing so, I can talk nicely and encourage

others too.

463. Just for Today, I won't judge others or myself. I'm not the "judge" and I don't have to be. Judging just hurts others and me and I don't want to do that anymore. Maybe I can try to understand instead of judging.

464. Just for Today, I will realize that I might not ever know something. Maybe I don't have to know to move forward.

465. Just for Today, I will not live in fear today or "depression". I'll sweep negative thoughts and emotions from my mind. I'm better than that. I'll do my best today and that is good enough.

466. Just for Today, I will consider whether I want to do something that will hurt me and/or someone else. I'll think it through before I act. I don't want to hurt others and I don't want to hurt myself.

467. Just for Today, I will consider whether something might be good before I reject what is in front of me today. Maybe it's good for me or for others and I don't know about it. I'll at least look at it and see if it is right for my children or me. I'll check it out further, if needed or wanted.

468. Just for Today, I will survive if others don't like me or approve of me. I am okay with myself and I am doing my best today. If "bruised", I will "pick myself up" and "get back into the game". No-one or no-thing is not going to get me down today.

469. Just for Today, I will realize that nothing is "black" and "white". There are always greys. There might even be some colors in there too! I'll expand my "vision" today to see the "bigger picture".

470. Just for Today, I will "create" my own world, days, holidays, etc. – within reason. I'll create my own enjoyment, goals, group of friends/family to be with, tasks, pleasures, etc. I'll

consider others in doing so and try to be flexible, though. This is <u>my</u> one and only life and I will try to live it as best as I can.

471. Just for Today, I will treat myself as well as I treat others.

472. Just for Today, I will realize that it's not all about me. I am one of many, yet I am one.

473. Just for Today, I will do "some thing(s)". These things sum up to make something.

474. Just for Today, I will pause – when I don't think I can take any more or I can't go any further. In those few seconds, you might find an internal burst of strength or insights on what to do next.

475. Just for Today, I will strive for better and progress. I will do things that make "it" better and/or I will make progress on "it".

476. Just for Today, I will not be hopeless. I will look for hope. Hope is what keeps me going.

477. Just for Today, I will find ways to keep on going when I am fearful, discouraged, etc. I will cheer myself on with good self-talk. I might do something religious or spiritual for strength to go on. I might seek comfort/support from others. I'll find ways to keep on going today – just for today.

478. Just for Today, I will believe in myself. I might believe in others and maybe even God, too. First, though, I will believe in myself – then go from there.

479. Just for Today, I will have self-confidence – at least enough to get through the day. I will continuously do things that build up my confidence as the day(s) go by.

480. Just for Today, I will not let my problems pile up. I'll deal with them as they occur, if possible. I'll not let my problems get me down. I'll seek help with my problems, if needed or wanted.

481. Just for Today, I will not become "emotionally unstable", if possible. I will manage my emotions and not let my emotions run my life. If I need help in managing my emotions and/or life, I will ask for help.

482. Just for Today, I will treasure "mental uplifts" as they occur in my day. If I need some uplifts, I'll look for them.

483. Just for Today, I will not try to do the "impossible". I will stick with realistic and achievable goals today.

484. Just for Today, I will try to be useful to others and myself. Being useful in life and having a purpose is good for me. I have to have something to live for – and I will find that.

485. Just for Today, I will not remain hopeless. I will look for hope for my current situation. I will be with people who spread hope instead of despair.

486. Just for Today, I will try to synchronize my body, mind, and spirit into one harmonic being.

487. Just for Today, I will seek out people who are like me instead of trying to fit in where I'm not wanted or needed. I also will have some people in my life who challenge my thinking and believing, since this is good for me.

488. Just for Today, I will be willing to make the effort.

489. Just for Today, I will be willing to accept help from others if wanted or needed. If I don't need or want help, I will tell them so.

490. Just for Today, I will try – at least try.

491. Just for Today, I will realize that I am not fully desperate. I will look for and be willing to consider my options. No matter what I decide to do or don't do, I am still a worthwhile person.

492. Just for Today, I will review my day and life occasionally to make sure I'm going in the right direction and being the person I want to be.

493. Just for Today, I will try to look at all the remedies around me for my current situation and decide then what to do or not do. I may have discarded a remedy in the past that might work now. I'll give it a try.

494. Just for Today, I will make peace with the religious/spiritual side of me. I'll decide what is best for me – and let others do the same for themselves. I don't want to fight with myself or anyone else about religion, spirituality, and/or God/Universe – or the lack thereof. I'll find something that works for me today. Some other day I might change my concepts, but for today, I will be at peace.

495. Just for Today, I will appreciate my body, mind, and spirit.

496. Just for Today, I will realize that no one or no thing is all good or all bad. I'll look for the good in everything and everyone.

497. Just for Today, I will discourage thoughts that "I am falling apart" or "the world is falling apart". Most of me and most of the world work well, most of the time. Today I'll make the most of what I have and be content with that.

498. Just for Today, I will let the world spin on its own. I don't have control of lots of things and people. I might as well just get used to it.

499. Just for Today, I will not be so cautious, fearful, and careful in living my day – afraid of what might happen. I'll just live today – and if something comes up, I will deal with it.

500. Just for Today, I will check my motives in thinking and acting around others. If I'm trying to get someone to do what they don't want to do, I'll stop right there – and mind my own business.

501. Just for Today, I will think of others more than myself. It's not good for me, or others, to think only of myself all the time.

502. Just for Today, I will try not to bully others into doing things

my way.

503. Just for Today, I will watch for others retaliating from my words or actions. I'll step back and see if I'm wrong. I, also, will not retaliate against others. I'll try to work things out calmly and peacefully. If not, I will just distance myself if possible.

504. Just for Today, I will see what I can contribute to life, the world, and others.

505. Just for Today, I will perform personal housecleaning – with the "physical debris" around me, with unhealthy relationships, and also with my "mental clutter".

506. Just for Today, I will try to be considerate of others.

507. Just for Today, I will make sure my actions match my words.

508. Just for Today, I will try to manage the obstacles in my life in one way or another.

509. Just for Today, I will try to have a good day, and a good life, with whatever I have or don't have.

510. Just for Today, I will make sure my priorities are right.

511. Just for Today, I will try to be cheerful and seek out humor in my day and my life.

512. Just for Today, I will try not to "overdo it" in anything and with anyone.

513. Just for Today, I will consider "help" in some way or another. Help might be good for me in the long run.

514. Just for Today, I will keep good habits and try to diminish/ stop old unhealthy habits.

515. Just for Today, I will try to be happy in my work.

516. Just for Today, I will realize that I have the rest of my life to live – and live I shall.

517. Just for Today, I will realize that no one or no thing is "perfect", including my work and me.

518. Just for Today, I will realize that I am "OK" no matter what

color I am, no matter how smart I am, no matter what my disability ...no matter what. I am OK just the way I am.

519. Just for Today, I will try to get a better outlook on my life. Maybe I don't have it so bad after all – or maybe I'm better off than I think.

520. Just for Today, I will try to work toward doing what I really want to do in life. I will take "one small step" toward that goal today.

521. Just for Today, I will just "jump in". Maybe it will be just fine once I get used to it. I might just think, "Why didn't I do this long ago?"

522. Just for Today, I will work toward getting myself out of something I don't want to be in – or is just too much for me. I might even ask for help in doing so.

523. Just for Today, I will take whatever life gives me today – and manage it. Some things I'll like and some things I probably won't. I'll make the best of what is given me today and what I have to work with.

524. Just for Today, I will realize I don't have to be alone. If I'm lonely, I'll do something about it. I'm not alone – unless I choose to be.

525. Just for Today, I will realize "I won't know until I get there".

526. Just for Today, I will seek out people I like and they like me. I will have a sense of belonging, of being wanted and needed. This is good.

527. Just for Today, I will look for similarities in those around me instead of differences. I will build on what we have in common.

528. Just for Today, I will stop staring at the problem(s) and instead look for a solution(s).

529. Just for Today, I will manage situations, when and if, they arise.

530. Just for Today, I will just keep on going.

531. Just for Today, I will stop to think before reacting to events/people/etc. After thinking, I will decide what I want or need to do – or not do.

532. Just for Today, I will grab onto hope with all my might – and I will give hope to others to do the same.

533. Just for Today, I will not feel sorry for myself, at least for not long. Instead, I'll work with what I do have and be grateful for that.

534. Just for Today, I will consider that my way of doing something might be a problem – for myself and/or maybe for others. Maybe I'm the problem and don't know it. Even if I don't want to, I'll step back and take a good look at myself.

535. Just for Today, I will do what I can up to the level of my abilities and energy – and maybe a little more, especially if it helps someone else.

536. Just for Today, I will realize that, in many cases, I don't have to do "what is expected of me". Sometimes I do, e.g. job, parent, etc. Other times, I'm just conforming to other's expectations, which I don't need to do. I'll decide moment by moment.

537. Just for Today, I will be gentle with myself and with others. If I need to get going, I'll gently encourage myself.

538. Just for Today, I will choose to be happy as much as I can. People and events might pull me away from being happy, but I will try to return to my new-normal happy state.

539. Just for Today, I will realize I might not always be successful. I'll give it a good try, though.

540. Just for Today, I will realize it's okay to make a mistake and more importantly admit my mistake(s).

541. Just for Today, I will realize that fixing the problems in my life might be an "inside job". I'll look "inside" for my "outside"

problems.

542. Just for Today, I will realize that I don't have to hurt myself with my unhealthy habits. I'll make better choices today. If I need help doing so, I will seek that out. I'm tired of being sick when I can do something about it.

543. Just for Today, I will consider that my physical symptoms might be a result of some psychological/emotional malfunctions. I'm like a computer in some ways with "hardware" and "software". Maybe my "software" is malfunctioning causing "hardware" symptoms.

544. Just for Today, I will try to find commonality with others rather than comparing myself to others or judging others. With everyone, there must be something we have in common. I'll build on that.

545. Just for Today, I will try to follow my own "moral compass" in deciding what to do or not do as the day goes on.

546. Just for Today, I will realize there is more to life than making money or my work. There is more to me than what I can do/accomplish in life – I am a person, too.

547. Just for Today, I will not let my goals determine my behavior. I'll not purposely hurt others to accomplish my goals or to make me feel good or look good.

548. Just for Today, I will try to maintain my integrity, self-esteem, and self-worth no matter what happens.

549. Just for Today, I will not fear rejection from the "outside" because I am okay with myself on the "inside".

550. Just for Today, I will try to improve or repair relationships with others and within myself.

551. Just for Today, I will just enjoy life.

552. Just for Today, I will not let my age determine what I do or don't do.

553. Just for Today, I will have a purpose – a reason for living – a

reason to get up, get dressed, and get on with the day.

554. Just for Today, I will try to know what I want to be – and what I don't want to be – and live accordingly.

555. Just for Today, I will realize that my performance does not determine my own individual self-worth or self-esteem.

556. Just for Today, I will try to understand others but maybe I need to understand myself first. Just a thought.

557. Just for Today, I will try not to "zone out" "veg out" too much, especially if it pulls me down. Instead, I'll shift my thinking to "daydreams" about my life and take actions to make my dreams possible.

558. Just for Today, I will not be bored too much. It's a waste of time. I have full power to change my thinking and get out of my rut. Today is a good day to start.

559. Just for Today, I will realize there is an "inside" everyone no matter what their "outside" looks like or acts like. Maybe their insides are much like my insides. I'll try to look beyond what I see and hear in a person.

560. Just for Today, I will realize it is my job to build my life the way I want it. No one else can do that for me. I might get help from others but it's up to me to try to make the effort.

561. Just for Today, I will try to finish things that I start – if I want to or need to. If I don't want to or need to do something, I'll consider not doing it or finishing it.

562. Just for Today, I will not let my diagnosis(s) determine my day or life. I may have limitations but I will work with those and have a good life nonetheless.

563. Just for Today, I will not think I'm dying or soon to die – unless it is true. There's more to life than getting ready to die.

564. Just for Today, I will not necessarily try to be like others just to "fit in". Instead, I'll be myself, be content with that, and be open to attracting others who like me just as I am.

565. Just for Today, I will consider whether it is important to me to "get ahead" in life. Maybe there are more important things to me than getting ahead.

566. Just for Today, I will be happy with what I have.

567. Just for Today, I will realize that everyone has good days and bad days, just like me. If I'm having a bad day, I'll try to turn it into a good day. There has to be something good about today – and I can find it and hold onto that.

568. Just for Today, I will not be a "magnet" for negativity or problems. If problems come up, I'll deal with them. If negativity occurs, I'll try to diminish or eliminate it.

569. Just for Today, I will consider that my life "survival skills" I picked up are maybe not needed anymore or not effective anymore.

570. Just for Today, I will realize that if something needs to change in my life then I'll change it – after thoughtful deliberation. My emotions will be an indicator of something that might need to change.

571. Just for Today, I will take care of the basics in life – good hygiene, eating right, sleeping right, and living right.

572. Just for Today, I will not be a "phony" to make sure people like me.

573. Just for Today, I will not do unhealthy things just to "fit in" with the crowd, because "everyone is doing it".

574. Just for Today, I will "grab hold of the moment/day" and act on my life instead of reacting to what life gives me.

575. Just for Today, I will be "okay" no matter what happens. I'll survive whatever happens and maybe I can learn from it.

576. Just for Today, I will realize I am responsible for myself – and my young children if I am a parent. Others are responsible for themselves.

577. Just for Today, I will not be afraid to die, e.g. the "Great

Unknown" – whether it is my time to die or not. I can live with uncertainty today. I'll do my best and let the rest go.

578. Just for Today, I will try to live a good life and let it go at that.

579. Just for Today, I will make sure my "word" is worth something.

580. Just for Today, I will realize "change" is part of life. As things and people change, I will continue to evaluate my options and act accordingly. Maybe this change will be good for me, I might ask myself.

581. Just for Today, I will strive for "quality of life" instead of "quantity of years". Maybe I can have both if I work for it.

582. Just for Today, I will maybe think it is time for me to "grow up". Then, again maybe it's a good day to act like a kid. Each day is different.

583. Just for Today, I will try to lead by example and make sure that my actions match my words.

584. Just for Today, I will try to be "available" to others instead of totally wrapped up in my own affairs/work.

585. Just for Today, I will strive for constructive activity, maybe especially to help others. Helping others helps me just as much, if not more, than helping others.

586. Just for Today, I will be free to laugh and I will be free to cry. I am free to express my emotions – I just gave myself permission to do so!

587. Just for Today, I will realize I am freer than what I think. Sometimes the only thing holding me back is myself. I want to be free – as free as I can be.

588. Just for Today, I will be okay with the psychological/ emotional side of me. It is a part of me just like my legs and arms.

589. Just for Today, I will consider that my thinking might be irrational. I'll at least consider it, especially if others bring it

to my attention.

590. Just for Today, I will try not to create problems of my own doing – for myself or for others. I'll think before I speak or act.

591. Just for Today, I will learn how to live with people. I might need help or special training, since I might not have these skills. Maybe my people skills need to be changed/revised/replaced with skills that actually work. I want to get along with people today and not be "at odds" with them.

592. Just for Today, I will live with whatever this day brings me and make the best of it.

593. Just for Today, I will learn life skills as wanted or needed. Learning new skills will help me cope with the demands of life better than my old ways.

594. Just for Today, I will try not to use "crutches" to get through this day or life in general. I might need some help in doing so, but I want to live life without the harmful crutches, e.g. excess alcohol, excess food, excess work, harmful drugs, etc.

595. Just for Today, I will look for the hope in each day.

596. Just for Today, I will try to make lifestyle changes as wanted or needed. I'll strive to make these changes life-long instead of just for the moment.

597. Just for Today, I will learn how to cope with the problems of life instead of hiding from them. I'll face life head-on today and see what happens. I can do it!

598. Just for Today, I will not dismiss the "soft side" of me – my thoughts, my emotions, etc. If necessary, I will seek help in "repairing" my thinking and my reactions to life.

599. Just for Today, I will consider that maybe, just maybe, I might need some improvement. Maybe the problems outside of me are related to my problems inside of me. I'll consider this and take heed today.

600. Just for Today, I will consider that I might be caring too much, probably in the wrong ways.

601. Just for Today, I will question my sense of impending troubles and dismiss these thoughts if there is no validity to them.

602. Just for Today, I will consider that I might need more than my own willpower to correct/stop unhealthy habits.

603. Just for Today, I will try not to be afraid of letting go of what I have to try something new. I'll also consider what I have to lose – which might not be much of anything. Maybe today is a good day to try something new.

604. Just for Today, I will try not to stagnate in my problems. I'll try to find and actually live working solutions.

605. Just for Today, I will consider changing my attitudes instead of trying to change the world.

606. Just for Today, I will try to accept life as it is in front of me today – and deal with it as best as I can. I might need some help doing so and I will consider that.

607. Just for Today, I will try not to criticize anyone or anything including myself.

608. Just for Today, I will try to look for and speak of the good in others and in the situations around me.

609. Just for Today, I will realize that I am one of many. Each of us and all of us have a right to live our own lives. I'll live my life and not meddle in others' lives.

610. Just for Today, I will just stop complaining and whining. Instead, I will try to be content with what I have and make the most of it.

611. Just for Today, I will consider that others might know more than I do and might be able to do a better job than what I can do.

612. Just for Today, I will try not to give advice to others, especially if they don't ask for my opinion. Even if they do

ask, I don't have to give my opinion if I don't feel comfortable doing so.

613. Just for Today, I will try at least to accept others as they are, and maybe even try to understand them better. I might even show some compassion, empathy, or maybe even love once I know the bigger picture around others.

614. Just for Today, I will try to add to life instead of seeing what I can get out of life.

615. Just for Today, I will try to get along with others. I might consider learning some new people skills, since my current ways sometimes don't seem to work very well.

616. Just for Today, I will realize that some people I will just not get along with very well, no matter how I or we try. Maybe it's just better to minimize contact and move on to those I do get along with better.

617. Just for Today, I will try not to have my expectations of life too high. I'll also try not to think of what I am entitled to from life, e.g. what life or others owe me. I want to be happy with what I have.

618. Just for Today, I will finally accept that others are going to do or not do what they want – whether I like it or not. Today I will not fret about what others should or shouldn't be doing – and just leave them alone – and instead focus on what I am doing or not doing today.

619. Just for Today, I will not try to change others who do not want to change.

620. Just for Today, I will let others be as long as they do not adversely affect me.

621. Just for Today, I will try to be friendly to others even if I don't feel like it.

622. Just for Today, I will just say "Thank You" when someone gives me something, even a compliment.

623. Just for Today, I will try and try again, making sure I'm going in the right direction.
624. Just for Today, I will keep what means most to me and let the rest go.
625. Just for Today, I will not try to fix something or someone that is okay as is.
626. Just for Today, I will not believe everything I hear or read and question what I see.
627. Just for Today, I will realize that my health is my most prized possession.
628. Just for Today, I will do what I need to do with the difficulties of the day.
629. Just for Today, I will take my health as it is and try to make it better.
630. Just for Today, I will make use of my good health to achieve my purpose. I need both health and purpose to live a good life.
631. Just for Today, I will try to keep myself healthy and happy – for my family, the world, and myself.
632. Just for Today, I will try to change before the pain gets too bad.
633. Just for Today, I will try to focus on good health instead of poor health.
634. Just for Today, I will try not to conjure up illness in my head based on flimsy information of what it could be or might be. I'll do what I can to become healthy and stay healthy – and leave it go at that.
635. Just for Today, I will be healthy until I get sick.
636. Just for Today, I will cry, if needed, and try to move on in my day.
637. Just for Today, I will try to focus on what I want instead of what I don't want around me today.

638. Just for Today, I will try to give what I can and maybe a little more if I'm up to it.

639. Just for Today, I will take "better" and "progress" in my life – and be grateful for that. If I'm having a better day, that's progress.

640. Just for Today, I will consider not wasting time and energy on things that don't mean anything to me. I'll focus on what is important to me today.

641. Just for Today, I will be cheerful, maybe humorous, to help others get their mind off their current bad situation. Sometimes holding their hand or other touches might help too. Prayer might help also. Since I can't fix them, maybe all I can do is to be there.

642. Just for Today, I will consider that I might have a problem or there is indeed a problem around me.

643. Just for Today, I will believe good things are going to happen.

644. Just for Today, I will try to go at my own speed even if others are going faster or slower than I am. I will consider whether my speed is affecting them adversely and if not, I will keep doing what I'm doing. Generally, I can go at my speed and others can go at their speed.

645. Just for Today, I will try to avoid gossiping since it might bring my mood down and it might hurt others. I don't want to hurt others and myself in my day.

646. Just for Today, I will have my own "space" around others. In my space, I will try to keep it clean, be positive, and be respectful of others. I might share my space with others if I want for a while – but afterward, I will return to my nice personal space for respite.

647. Just for Today, I will try to focus on something else if some other thing or person is bothering me.

648. Just for Today, I will realize it's only for today.

649. Just for Today, I will try to help others and not "bug" them.
650. Just for Today, I will realize I'm never alone, unless I choose to be.
651. Just for Today, I will let others "do it themselves" for the most part. That is best for both others and me. I might think of cheering them on if appropriate.
652. Just for Today, I will realize today is one day of probably many more. I'll do what I can today but there is always tomorrow too.
653. Just for Today, I will try not to "pick a fight" with my words or actions. I don't want or need that in my life. If I'm in a bad mood, I'll work on that, instead of lashing out at others.
654. Just for Today, I will realize that sometimes I just don't "fit in" with a certain group. I'll not waste my time and energy trying to fit in where I'm not wanted or needed. I'll find others who do want and need me in their lives.
655. Just for Today, I will try not to control others by words or actions, unless it is my job to do so. I'll consider my motives when I want to control and if it is just to get people to do it my way, I'll stop right there. In that case, I need an attitude adjustment and let others be.
656. Just for Today, I will try to be aware of others around me – how my words and actions might adversely affect them. I want to do no harm today – to others or myself.
657. Just for Today, I will try not to have the day "rule" me, especially if it is a holiday. I can have the best day I can and others can do the same – with or without me.
658. Just for Today, I will pause my day occasionally to zoom out and look at the "bigger picture" of my day. If I don't like what I see, I'll change it mid-stream and take a new course for the day.
659. Just for Today, I will realize that others are others and that's

okay. I'll be me.

660. Just for Today, I will give others and events a fair chance. I'll try to look for the good in them. I'll try not to judge, especially prematurely.

661. Just for Today, I will dare to live without the confines of my past.

662. Just for Today, I will stop imagining that I'm holding up others, that I'm not good enough, that my work is not good enough, etc. Today, I will deal only with reality and not my faulty thinking. If I need to check something out, I will do so. Otherwise, I'll just do my day and try to minimize the nagging voices inside me.

663. Just for Today, I will relax and have faith that today is a good day.

664. Just for Today, I will just stop my busy-ness and ask myself "Why am I doing this?" I'm hurting others and myself with my busy-ness.

665. Just for Today, I will realize I don't have to join in with others if I don't want to. What they're doing might just not appeal to me, be uncomfortable to me, or beyond my limits.

666. Just for Today, I will maybe not look for an end to my current situation, but rather look for a change – in me, my attitudes, improvement, progress, etc.

667. Just for Today, I will consider that a solution(s) might come in a way I hadn't expected. I'll "keep an eye open" for all possible solutions today.

668. Just for Today, I will decide how much other's words and actions are going to affect me. The same goes for events – I'll decide what to do, or not do, as each event happens.

669. Just for Today, I will consider that others might not realize they're "doing it" – whatever "it" is. They're probably not doing it to irritate me. I'll try to ignore them doing "it" and

go about my own business.

670. Just for Today, I will realize that some days are just "messy" and not going the way I had planned. I'll still continue adapting to "what is" and look for the good in this messy day.

671. Just for Today, I will remember that I can speak up for myself. It is my responsibility to act on my own behalf, not expecting someone else to do it for me, or expecting others to automatically know what I'm thinking or feeling.

672. Just for Today, I will not accept others hurting me just because "that's the way they are".

673. Just for Today, I will try to be patient with others and myself.

674. Just for Today, I will try not to get in other's way. Instead, I'll go my way and let them go their way. If we have commonality, I might try to create a new friendship.

675. Just for Today, I will continue to do what I think is important, as long as I don't hurt others – because it is important to me. Others might not think of my efforts as important and that's okay – they have a right to their opinion as much as I do.

676. Just for Today, I will try to rein in my thinking from "what's next" to what I'm doing now. I can't do a good job if my mind is elsewhere (distracted).

677. Just for Today, I will consider that if "it" is okay with others, I can be okay with it too. I might not think it is okay what they are doing or not doing, but I'll just let them be as long as it doesn't adversely affect me personally. I'll try to "Mind my own Business".

678. Just for Today, I will not be so tied to the time, checking the clock frequently. This just stresses me out. I'll check the time as needed, not because I'm driven to do so.

679. Just for Today, I will consider that if "it" bothers me more than others, maybe I'm over-reacting, imagining something

that is not true, or "making something out of nothing".

680. Just for Today, I will accept that I just can't stop or do anything about some things/people. For example, I can't stop the passage of time; I can't change the past; I can't change people who don't want to change themselves; etc.

681. Just for Today, I will try to have my day/life balanced and not revolve around a particular person or situation. I'll do a little bit of this and a little bit of that. If I get "out of balance", I will pause, get perspective, and try to re-center myself.

682. Just for Today, I will finally get the message that some people just don't want to hear what I have to say – and that's okay. I'll not be a pest today to others. I'll be okay with and within myself – and be open to those who are interested in what I have to say and what I am doing.

683. Just for Today, I will realize I don't have to "fix" everything and everyone. I will also realize there are some things and some people that I just can't fix. I'll try to be okay with leaving some things and people "undone".

684. Just for Today, I will not try to plan other's day for them, with my priorities, my agenda, and my timeline. Others have a right to their own day without me interfering.

685. Just for Today, I will try to "let things happen" instead of "making things happen" so much. If it doesn't fit, maybe I need to change my strategy instead of trying to try to make it fit.

686. Just for Today, I will realize there will always be "loose ends", even if I don't like it. Maybe I can get used to life's loose ends, instead of stressing out over them.

687. Just for Today, I will manage the pain(s) in my life and not have my pain(s) manage my day and me.

688. Just for Today, I will think before I speak or act considering whether it is worth saying or doing, considering my stress in

doing so, and whether it would do any good.

689. Just for Today, I will give my best to others, smile at others, and compliment/encourage others.

690. Just for Today, I will ask others before I try to help. If they clearly say no, I will not go ahead and try to help them anyhow. Today, I will respect others, as well as myself.

691. Just for Today, I will consider accepting help from others. I might not like to do so, but maybe help is necessary for me to have a good day.

692. Just for Today, I will be careful to make sure help offered to me is a gift or paid for – and not come with hidden "strings attached". If I'm not sure, I'll ask.

693. Just for Today, I will try to relax when I am with family, friends, or in other groups. I'll try to be just me and not "try so hard". I'll just "chill out" and enjoy it.

694. Just for Today, I will do and be my best – if that's not good enough, I'll ask myself "Why am I here?"

695. Just for Today, I will respect what is important to others – as well as respecting what is important to me.

696. Just for Today, I will remember that I don't have to react/engage with every person and event in my day. I'll respond to what happens today and maybe do more or less, if I need or want to.

697. Just for Today, I will try not to be driven to help/fix others. I'll do what I can today. If others want to do more, I'll not get in their way.

698. Just for Today, I will get used to the fact that others have different priorities than mine – and we might not agree on what to do next. I'll try to harmonize my priorities with others, as much as possible.

699. Just for Today, I will remember that not "everything" is my fault. I'll not take on all the troubles of the world as my own

personal responsibility.

700. Just for Today, I will accept my part in adverse events, maybe make amends, and try to resolve the situation as best as I can – then I will move on and try not to make the same mistake in the future.

701. Just for Today, I will keep doing the right things.

702. Just for Today, I will not hide from potential, or even inevitable, losses. I will fully participate in life and accept losses as part of life. I will think of the gains more than the losses.

703. Just for Today, I will consider that I don't know everything. Maybe I could set aside what I think I know and be open to new information, insights, people, etc.

704. Just for Today, I will consider that death might not be what I think it is. I guess I don't get a choice when it is my time to die, so I will try to be open to death – but not think too much about it until then! In the meantime, I will live!

705. Just for Today, I will slow down my body and mind. All I seem to do is hurt myself, and maybe others, by rushing around, eating too fast, not taking enough time in the bathroom, ending conversations prematurely, etc. Most of the time there is no need to rush.

706. Just for Today, I will consider that it might not be good for me to "get it out in the open", "get it off my chest", "just blurt it out", confess my "sins", "come clean", etc. – if it might cause more harm to others/relationships than do good. I'll think carefully before I speak or act today.

707. Just for Today, I will just say that I have enough information today. It is time to "do" instead of seeking or wallowing in more and more information.

708. Just for Today, I will try to say something good about a person or situation.

709. Just for Today, I will face up to my reality, whatever it is. I'll not look for trouble. If I have troubles, I will deal with them, not hide from them. At least I can make a start today.

710. Just for Today, I will try not to force situations or people. I can hurt other people and myself by forcing, coercing, pushing, etc.

711. Just for Today, I will realize there is only so much I can do for a person, situation, etc. The rest is up to them.

712. Just for Today, I will realize that life is not "one size fits all", especially when it gets into "my way is good for all". Everyone handles life their own way and I want to respect that and them. If I do that, it is better for them, for me, and for relationships.

713. Just for Today, I will think of others but I will also think of myself, too. How am I doing in all this? Is there something I need to do to take care of myself first? – Especially before I try to help others.

714. Just for Today, I will realize that everyone sees things differently. One example, of many, is that some people like holidays and some don't. My view of life is as good as their view of life. If their view looks better than mine does, however, I might switch over to their view.

715. Just for Today, I will maintain my own "self" no matter how close I am to another. If I am in a group, I will remember that I am still an individual in the group – I am not the group.

716. Just for Today, I will not tease, joke around at the expense of others, make fun of others, ridicule, tell offensive jokes, etc. I want to respect others as much as I respect myself.

717. Just for Today, I will realize that sometimes my "best guess" is as good as it gets. Maybe my best guess will get the job done, probably a lot faster and better than waiting for a perfect solution to come along – if it ever does.

718. Just for Today, I will look at the "at least's" in my day and life – e.g. at least I'm alive, at least part of my home is okay, at least it's better than it was, at least I have my health, etc.

719. Just for Today, I will think about something else or do something else when negative or troublesome thoughts linger in my mind preventing me from having the best day I can.

720. Just for Today, I will ask others what they want – instead of assuming that I know what they want – or worse yet, deciding for them what they want.

721. Just for Today, I will also consider what is best for others, or the "whole", instead of just thinking of what is best for me.

722. Just for Today, I will try not to get "stuck" or stay "stuck". I'll take actions to get unstuck and move on.

723. Just for Today, I will tether myself to today and now. I might drift off into the future or the past, but I will rein myself in to what is right in front of me now.

724. Just for Today, I will try to be positive, talk positively, and act positively. This is good for me and for others around me to do so.

725. Just for Today, I will talk and think about something else other than sickness, death, aches/pains, my problems, or the problems of the world. There is more to me than problems – and I want to be more than problems.

726. Just for Today, I will check whether what is bothering me is real or imagined. If needed or wanted, I can check with others, too, on this. No sense getting bothered over imagined troubles.

727. Just for Today, I will just slow down, e.g. eating, going to the bathroom, running all over, etc. All I do when I go too fast is make mistakes and maybe hurt myself/others.

728. Just for Today, I will "live and learn" from my mistakes and also from other's mistakes. "Close Calls" can be a "wake up

call" to change my behavior, e.g. driving habits, near accidents working, etc.

729. Just for Today, I will remember that I don't have to make the same mistakes others make. I can learn from them how to "stay out of trouble".

730. Just for Today, I will remember that some/most things I worry about never happen – so I'll just not worry today.

731. Just for Today, I will realize that others do not go at my speed. Some go faster and some go slower. Is it worth the stress trying to get others to go my speed? Maybe I can change my speed or adapt to their speed more.

732. Just for Today, I will consider that when "I feel bad for or about...." - whether my feelings are out of sympathy/empathy or whether my feelings are out of guilt. If my feelings are out of guilt I will try to figure out some way not to feel guilty about what is going on around me.

733. Just for Today, I will take/do some actions so that I don't feel "sick and tired".

734. Just for Today, I will remember that I don't have to "fill in the silence" when I'm around others. Silence is okay. I don't have to "make conversation" when I really don't want to or have anything to say.

735. Just for Today, I will try not to be so fussy, finicky, difficult, demanding when there is no good reason to be. All this does is create undue stress in my relationships and me.

736. Just for Today, I will not feel like I have to say "I'm sorry" for every little thing that goes on. If I truly did something wrong I'll apologize – otherwise I'll suppress myself in apologizing all the time. I'm worth more than that.

737. Just for Today, I will consider whether my beliefs might be hurting others and myself. Maybe my beliefs are outdated and don't fit me anymore.

738. Just for Today, I will remember that many things/people "heal" on their own. Healing might happen faster and better if the source(s) of harm is diminished or removed though.

739. Just for Today, I will realize that life is a series of "New Normals". That's just how life is and I can deal with these changes or maybe I don't have to do anything. I'll figure it out as I go today.

740. Just for Today, I will be honest with others who want/expect more out of me than what I can or want to give. I'll not "string them along" with silence, maybe's, or other indirect messages.

741. Just for Today, I will listen more to what people are saying instead of preparing in my head what I'm going to say next. I really want to "listen" to what people say today.

742. Just for Today, I will believe that somehow, someway, somewhere "it" will work out. I want to be open to answers, solutions, etc. today – in whatever form they may appear.

743. Just for Today, I will choose to have hope instead of being hopeless.

744. Just for Today, I will allow myself to "get my hopes up". I want to be ready for when the solutions come.

745. Just for Today, I will remember that life will go on despite what happens or doesn't happen.

746. Just for Today, I will try to do no additional harm if I have harmed in some way already.

747. Just for Today, I will realize that everyone has problems, difficulties, issues, troubles, worries, messes, etc. – even if I can't see it from the outside.

748. Just for Today, I will try not to add to other's problems.

749. Just for Today, I will stop occasionally and let my senses absorb what is going on around me.

750. Just for Today, I will be free to imagine "God" and the

"Afterlife" the way I want to and not be confined by what I think I know, what I was taught, and/or what I was shown.

751. Just for Today, I will purposely not ruin someone else's good day.

752. Just for Today, I will not rob someone else's dignity, crushing their self-esteem, by my words or actions.

753. Just for Today, I will trust that "they" are okay and "it" is okay.

754. Just for Today, I will trust that whatever happens, I will be able to handle it – no matter what. If I need or want help in managing, I will ask for it.

755. Just for Today, I will not move my "finish lines" in a job or project just to add more items. If others try to do so, I will speak up and negotiate a new project timeline/price based on the added items.

756. Just for Today, I will not let my few "wrongs" overpower many of the things I do right. Everyone makes mistakes. I'll learn from my wrongs and try not to do them again – but I will not dwell on them.

757. Just for Today, I will avoid bringing up other's mistakes from the past. I have enough to do just handling my own mistakes.

758. Just for Today, I will be healthy. I will eat right, sleep right, exercise moderately, stay sober, live right, and avoid unhealthy activities or thoughts. This is good for me and for my family.

759. Just for Today, I will choose to do some good things for myself and some good things for others. I'll not forget to be good to myself in my haste to be good to others.

760. Just for Today, I will realize there is a limit to my responsibility in any situation. I'm not fully responsible for everything and for everyone. I will attend to my part of the responsibility and not take on the whole load.

761. Just for Today, I will remember that I am okay in and of

myself. No one can take that away from me.

762. Just for Today, I will listen to and absorb constructive criticism/feedback as an adult, and not react like a defensive child. If their comments are valid, I will negotiate a workable improvement plan for myself. I will not, however, tolerate destructive criticism meant only to hurt me.

763. Just for Today, I will remember I don't have to be like others. I can choose to be like others if I want or need to though.

764. Just for Today, I will live in my own life and not try to climb into someone else's life. It works best if everyone lives their own life. If I don't like my life, I will take actions to change it.

765. Just for Today, I will remember that usually I can back out of situations or back away from certain people if I need or want to.

766. Just for Today, I will get used to the fact that life and people are often not logical.

767. Just for Today, I will remember I can go back to what was working then that I'm not doing now.

768. Just for Today, I will be my own "new me". Others might not like the "new me" but I do. I will respect others, however, and let them be. If I want to change the "new me" I can do so at any time. I want to grow and change as needed or wanted.

769. Just for Today, I will realize that there is probably no emergency and no one is pushing me – except me. I'll slow down, take the pressure off, and continue in my day.

770. Just for Today, I will get a life of my own.

771. Just for Today, I will grieve losses in my life as needed or wanted.

772. Just for Today, I will just say that today is good enough.

773. Just for Today, I will enlist help as needed or wanted, especially if I just can't do it all myself.

774. Just for Today, I will have limits on how much I help others –

considering my responsibility to take care of myself and my family first. I will let them know how much I can help and just do that much. The rest is up to them. I can't do it all – I can only do so much.

775. Just for Today, I will be okay, despite what is going on around me.

776. Just for Today, I will avoid thoughts like ("Look at me". "See how good I am compared to *those* people", etc.) I'll especially not verbalize these thoughts to others. It's probably better if I just avoid comparing myself with others altogether.

777. Just for Today, I will keep moving, keep learning, keep growing, keep searching, and just keep going.

778. Just for Today, I will consider "nudging" someone who seems to be struggling, perhaps by sharing my experiences to show them they're not alone.

779. Just for Today, I will not let pride and stubbornness keep me from doing the right thing.

780. Just for Today, I will finish something and move on – or not finish something and move on. I'll carefully consider what to do or not do.

781. Just for Today, I will not underestimate or "blow-off" people or situations around me.

782. Just for Today, I will remember that the phone "works both ways". If I'm lonely or caring about someone, I'll call them instead of waiting for them to call me.

783. Just for Today, I will try to be a good "team player" in whatever team I'm in, e.g. work-life, sports, relationships, etc. I'll be honest with my team to let them know what I can and cannot/will not do, so they know what to expect from me.

784. Just for Today, I will not wait too long to take care of important things, e.g. going to the bathroom, fixing the car, seeing the doctor, etc.

785. Just for Today, I will manage the possible guilt feelings associated with taking care of loved ones and myself first – instead of putting others first and my loved ones/myself second. If I need emotional support/therapy, I will do so. Others might not like this but it is very important to me to take care of my immediate family and myself first.

786. Just for Today, I will periodically ask myself – "Is what I'm gaining in this day and my life worth what I'm losing?" If I'm losing what is really important to me in life by questing for more gain in something – I'll stop right there and go back to what is truly important to me.

****

How about you? What are your "Just for Today's" that could help you Manage the Stressors in your life – instead of letting life "run you ragged"?

1. Just for Today, I will

_____ ;

2. Just for Today, I will

_____ ;

3. Just for Today, I will

_____ ;

4. Just for Today, I will

_____ ;

5. Just for Today, I will

_____ .

Take-Aways

- You and I can do something, even if it is something we don't want to do – "Just for Today";

- We can choose how we live, think, and act today – "Just for Today";
- We can live our own lives and let others live theirs – "Just for Today".

Chapter 3 – Conclusion

Unpondering all that I've written, all I can say is that when I follow my Guidelines I feel better about myself and others. I seem to get along better with others too. My Guidelines give me direction and purpose in life - It works for me.

Epilogue and Attributions

I hope what I have given you in this book helps you in some way.

It really helped me to get my thoughts and feelings out on paper – to write about them. As I was writing, I was thinking that my efforts might help someone, which made me feel good.

At the time of this writing, I'm 73 years old. Maybe in years to come, I'll revise my book, since I'm a "work in progress". I'm always learning and there's always "room for improvement". I just want to be the best Tom I can be in this life on a daily basis. Who knows about the next life? ☺

I wish you all well.

Tom

Thanks to Canva[1] for the wonderful Design Tool, my Publishers, Microsoft Word, my Personal Life Experiences, the Universe for providing Information and Guidance in writing this book, and most importantly to you for reading this book.

The End (of this book)

****

Tom Garz - TG Ideas LLC[2]
691 S. Green Bay Rd. # 180
Neenah, WI 54956 U.S.A.
E-Mail tgideas@gmail.com

---

1.   https://www.canva.com/

2. https://sites.google.com/site/tgideas/

Don't miss out!

Visit the website below and you can sign up to receive emails whenever Tom Garz publishes a new book. There's no charge and no obligation.

https://books2read.com/r/B-A-BDUH-UVJLB

BOOKS 2 READ

Connecting independent readers to independent writers.

Also by Tom Garz

Paging Dr. Within: How to Become, Be, and/or Make a "Patient Listener" and/or a "Super Symptom Checker"
Coronavirus-The Inside Story: Multidimensional Prevention and Treatment
Living Through This Pandemic: "Just for Today"
Over 700 Ways to Live "Just for Today"

About the Author

Tom Garz is the manager of TG Ideas LLC - writing and inventing, since 2003.

"Helping to make this a better world by providing information to others on what has been done already and offer up ideas on what else might be done"

Tom has a technical background, a B.S. in Physics, and has worked in variety of jobs in his life. He always has had an interest in Electronics and "fringe science". "Exploring" is one of his favorite activities. Tom has a keen interest in writing and inventing.

Tom hopes you find his books beneficial for you and/or others. :-)

Tom might be available as a Consultant. Contact TG Ideas LLC, if interested.

tgideas@gmail.com

About the Publisher

TG Ideas LLC is a limited liability company registered in Wisconsin. It was formed in Spring of 2003.

The Mission of TG Ideas LLC is to "Help make this a better world by providing information to others on what has been done already and offer up ideas on what else might be done"

TG Ideas does not make or sell any products, other than publications. Tom Garz, of TG Ideas LLC, might be available as a Consultant. Contact - tgideas@gmail.com

https://sites.google.com/site/tgideas/

Made in the USA
Las Vegas, NV
27 February 2021